First Facts

Energy from Oil and Gas

DONNA BAILEY

HEINEMANN

How to use this book

This book tells you lots of things about oil and natural gas. There is a list of Contents on the next page. It shows you what each double page of the book is about. For example, pages 12 and 13 tell you about 'How we find oil and gas'.

On all of these pages you will find some words that are printed in **bold** type. The bold type shows you that these words are in the Glossary on pages 46 and 47. The Glossary explains the meaning of some words which may be new to you.

At the very end of the book there is an Index. The Index tells you where to find certain words in the book. For example, you can use it to look up words like hydrocarbons, fossil fuels, seismic survey and many other words to do with oil and natural gas.

Material used in this book first appeared in Macmillan World Library: *Oil and Natural Gas*.
Published by Heinemann Children's Reference
A division of Heinemann Educational Books Ltd
Halley Court, Jordan Hill, Oxford OX2 8EJ

British Library Cataloguing in Publication data
Bailey, Donna

Energy from oil and gas
1. Natural gas and petroleum
I. Title II. Series
553.2′8

ISBN 0 431 00906 6

Printed in Hong Kong

Contents

Introduction

When this plane takes off its engines
are at full power.
The engines are using lot of **energy**.

The engines get the energy by burning the fuel stored in the plane's wings.

You can see and feel energy as heat, light and movement and it can change from one form of power to another.

People and animals get energy from food and turn it into movement. When wood burns, the energy stored in it changes into heat and light.

Most of the world's energy comes from oil, gas, wood and coal, but we also get energy from wind and water power.

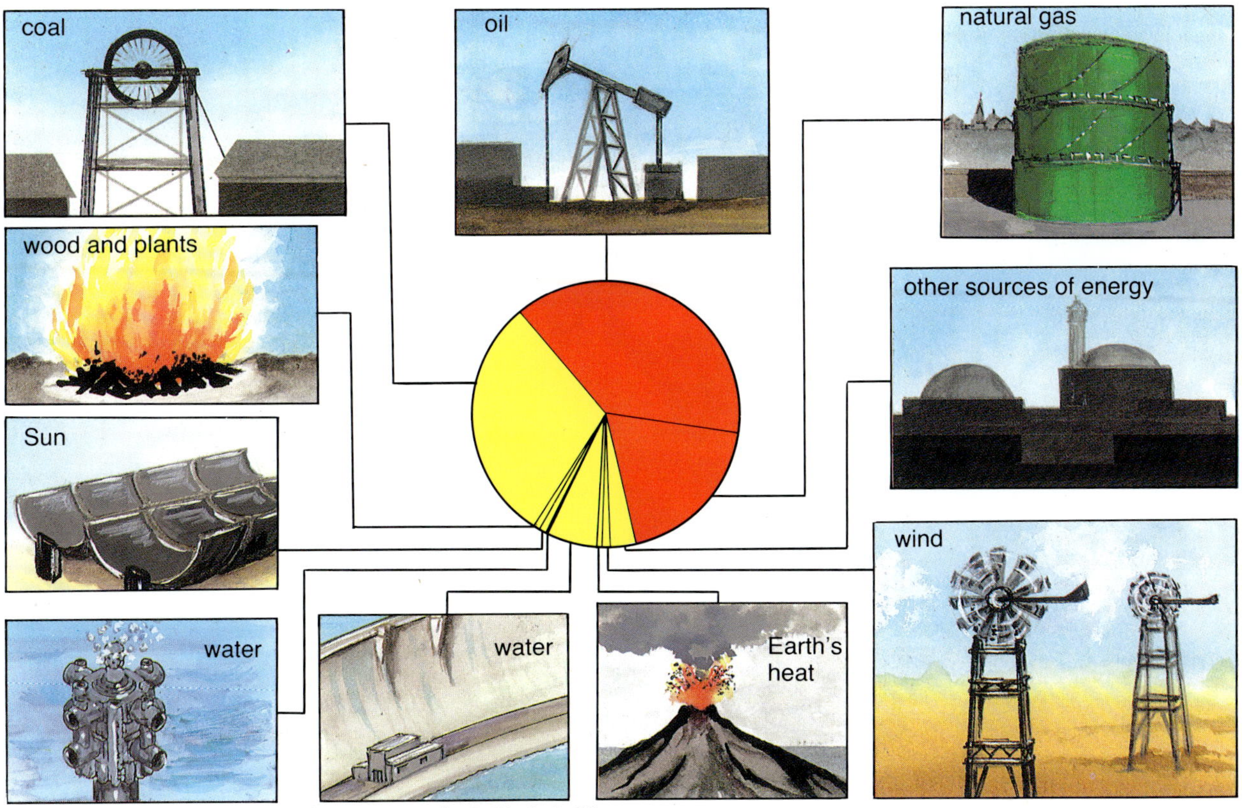

Fuels in the Earth

Coal, oil and natural gas all come from the remains of plants and animals which lived millions of years ago. Oil and gas come from the remains of tiny sea plants and animals, like the plankton in our picture.

The plankton took in heat and light from the Sun. They used the gas **carbon dioxide** to change the heat and light into food.

When the plankton died, they fell on to the seabed and were covered by thick layers of sand and mud. Over millions of years the layers of mud and sand turned into hard rock.

The bodies of plants and animals contain **oxygen, hydrogen** and **carbon.** When the plankton died, oxygen left their bodies. The remaining carbon and hydrogen in their bodies turned into **hydrocarbons.**

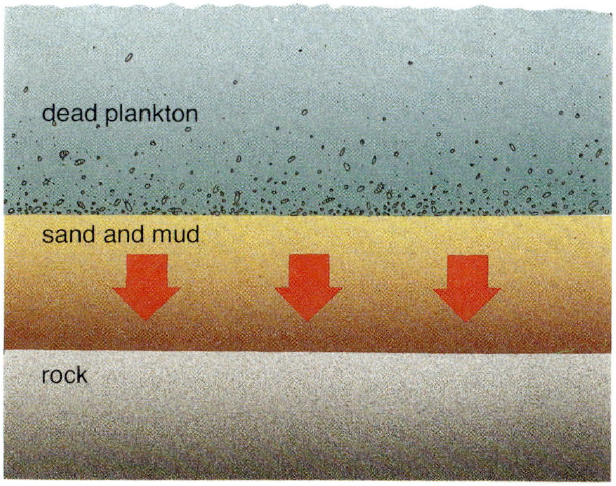

dead trees and animals sank to the bottom of the prehistoric swamps

How oil and gas were made

By looking at **fossils** we can find out about the plants and animals that lived millions of years ago.
After millions of years the hydrocarbon remains of the tiny plankton in the rocks turned into **fossil fuels**.
Some fossil fuels made a thick liquid called oil and others formed natural gas.

The layers of rocks slowly built up over millions of years.
Heavy rocks pressed down on the fossil fuels and squeezed water, oil and gas out of the softer rocks.
The oil and gas became trapped in between layers of harder rocks.

Today, **drills** from oil rigs are used to cut through the rocks.

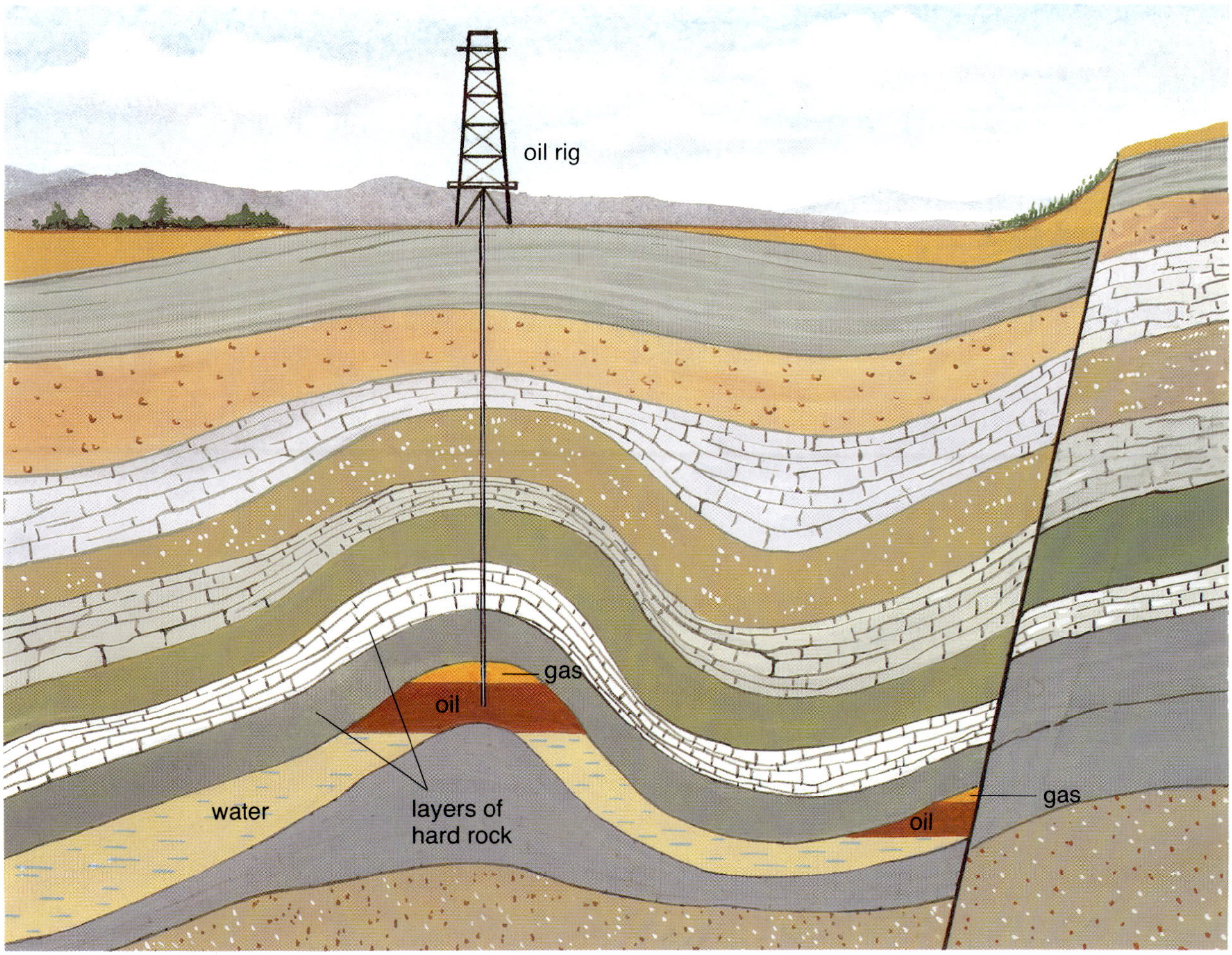

Finding oil long ago

Nearly 2000 years ago the Chinese used a pointed stone to dig deep holes in the ground.
They were looking for rock salt.
The Chinese were the first people to discover oil under the earth.

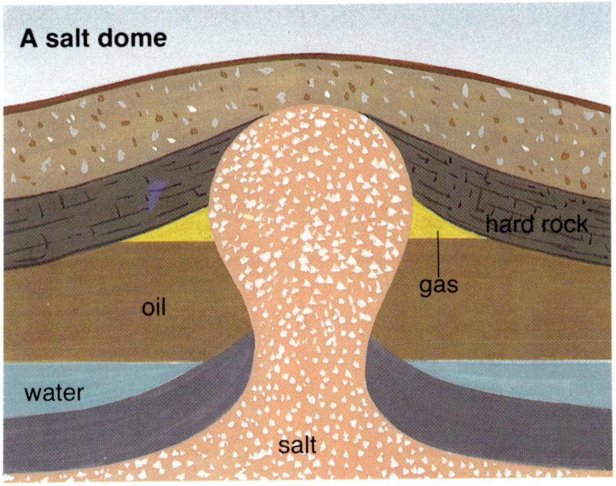

Our diagram shows how a dome of rock salt has pushed through other rocks. Oil and gas cannot pass through the hard rock salt.

When the Chinese dug for salt, they found oil too.

Oil helps the parts of machines to move smoothly. When people began to use more machines they needed more oil.

Edwin Drake was the first American to drill for oil. In 1859 he found oil at a place called Titusville. Lots of other people began to drill for oil in the same place, in Pennsylvania. Soon there were hundreds of oil wells in the United States.

oil wells in the United States in 1869

How we find oil and gas

Oil companies use **geologists** to help them find oil underground in the rocks. The geologists find a place which they think might have the right kinds of rocks where they can find oil.
The geologists clear away the trees and make a **seismic survey** of the land. They set off a series of small explosions in the ground.

Instruments called **geophones** pick up **shock waves** from the explosions. The shock waves bounce off hard rocks underground. Scientists in a survey truck measure the waves. They can tell from these measurements if the rocks under the ground hold oil.

a scientist colours a map of the underground rocks

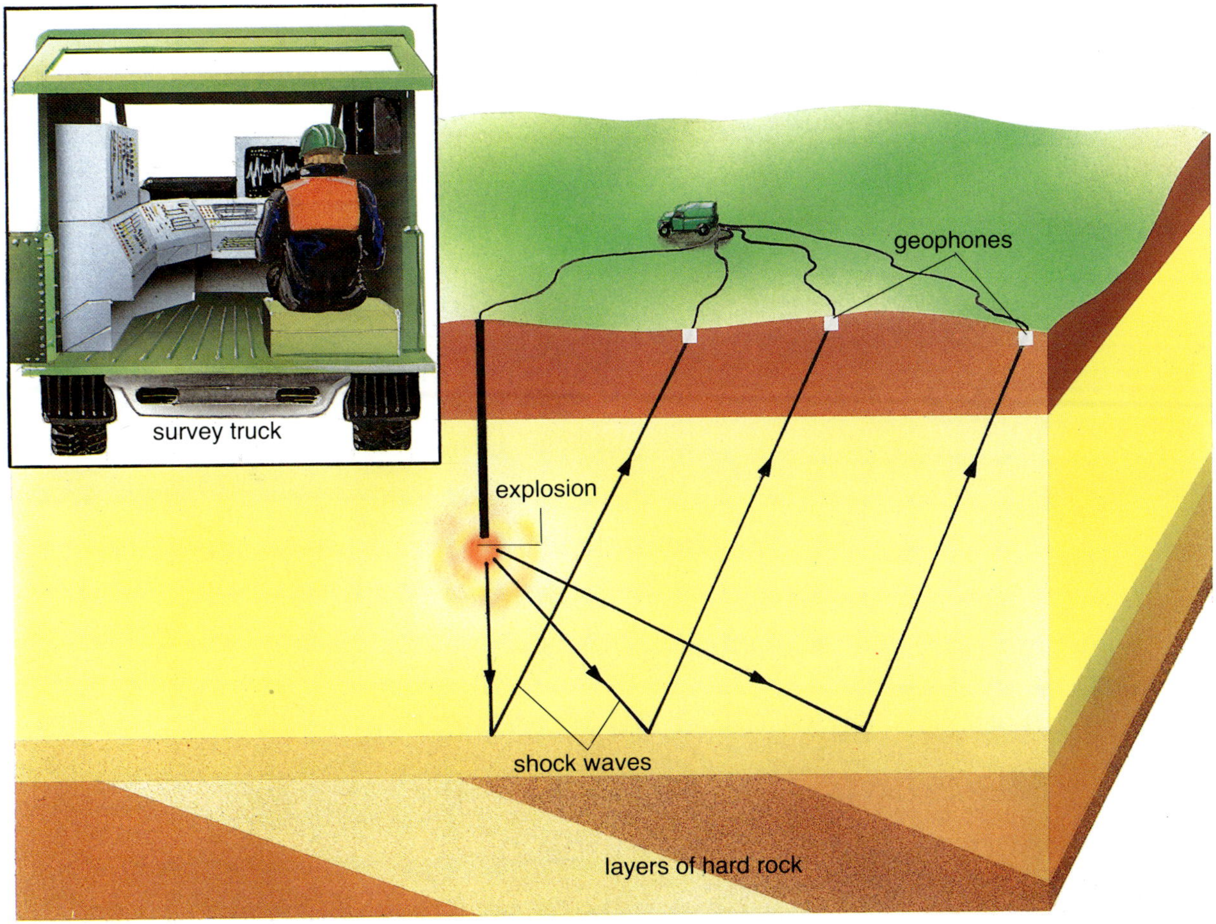

Searching from the air

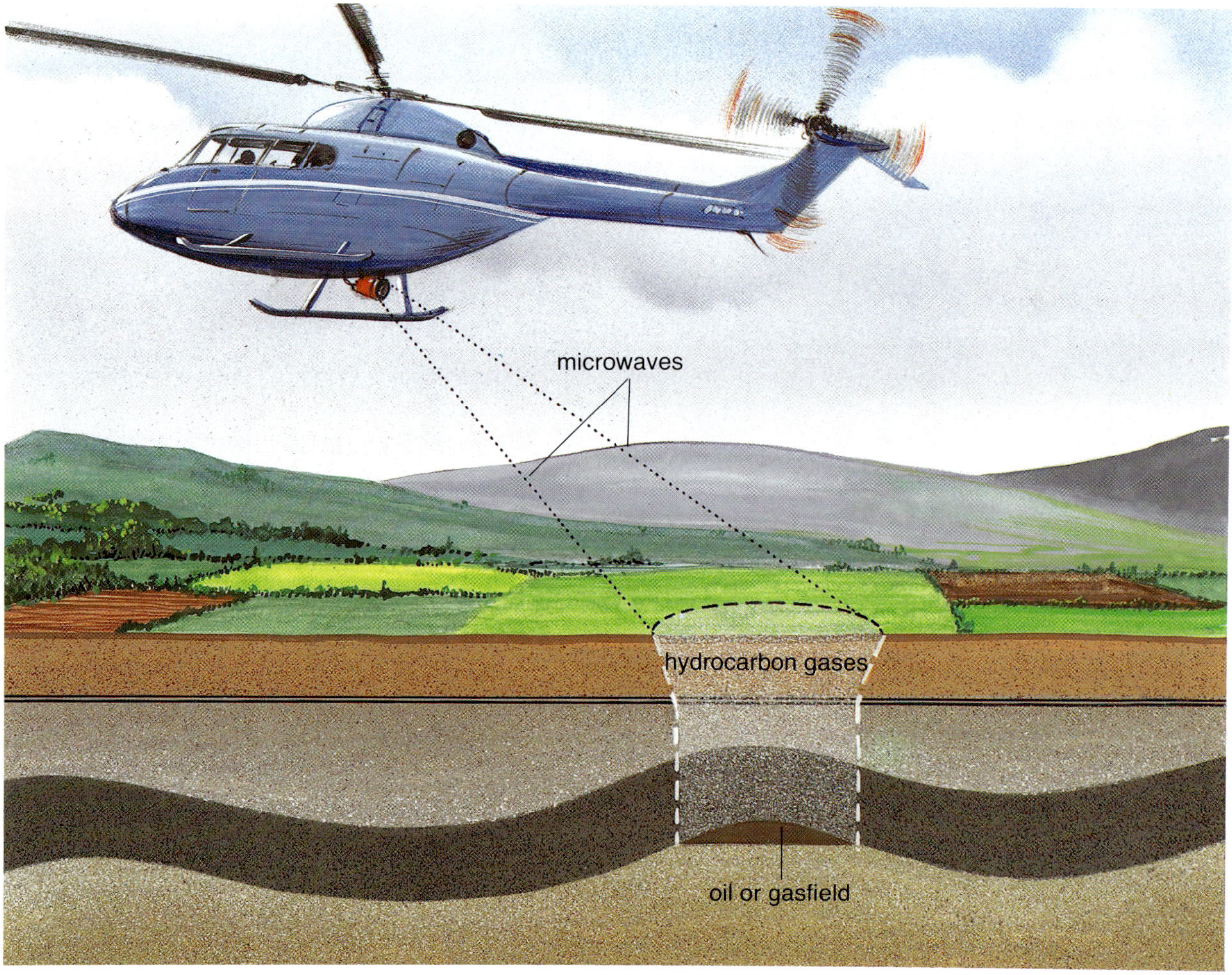

Geologists often use helicopters to look for oil or gas beneath the ground. They use a machine which sends out special rays called **microwaves**. Microwaves can 'sniff out' any hydrocarbon gases in the air. These gases show where to find oil.

a space satellite

Geologists also take photographs from aircraft. They use special **infra-red** cameras or they take infra-red **satellite** photographs. These photographs show shapes under the ground in different colours.
The geologists make maps from these photographs.

an infra-red photograph

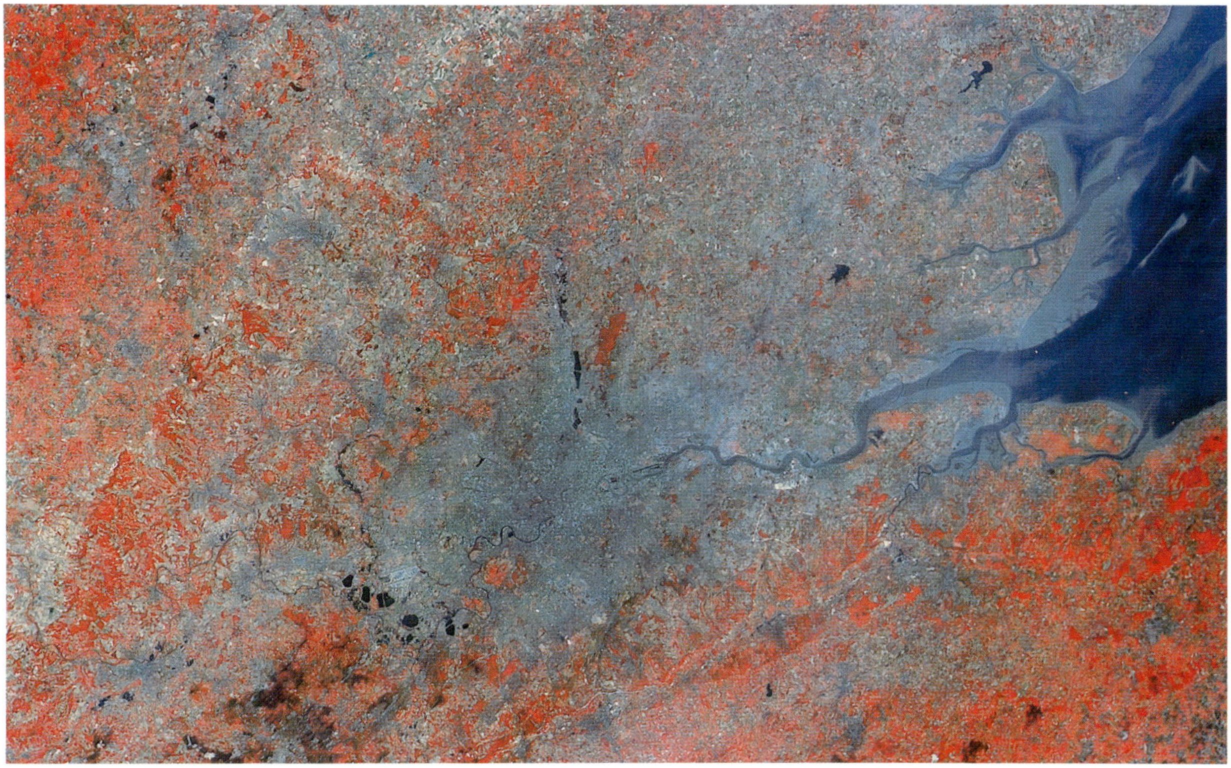

A test well

It costs an oil company a lot of money to drill for oil, so the workers drill a test well first to make sure they have found somewhere with plenty of oil.

The engineers build a **derrick** to hold the heavy drill and all the long pipes that go deep into the ground. The derrick must be tall and strong.

a test well in Nigeria

Drilling is easier on land. If the drill site is under water the oil workers must build a **drilling platform**. Then teams of oil workers work day and night, drilling for oil.

The drill brings samples of rock up to the surface. The geologists study these samples to find out how much oil there is under the ground.

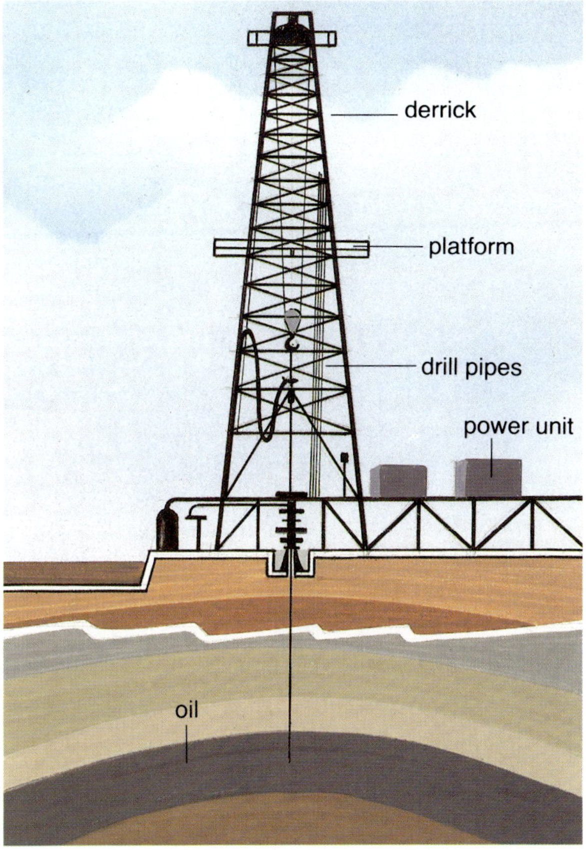

a test well on land

geologists found no oil at a test site on this farm

Drilling for oil

Workers on an oil rig are sometimes called **roughnecks**.
Their work is hard and often boring.
They do the same job over and over again when they dig an oil well.

The workers fit a pipe nine metres long to the drill.
They drill nine metres into the ground.
Then they add another bit of pipe and drill, and so on.

adding drill pipes

drilling through rock

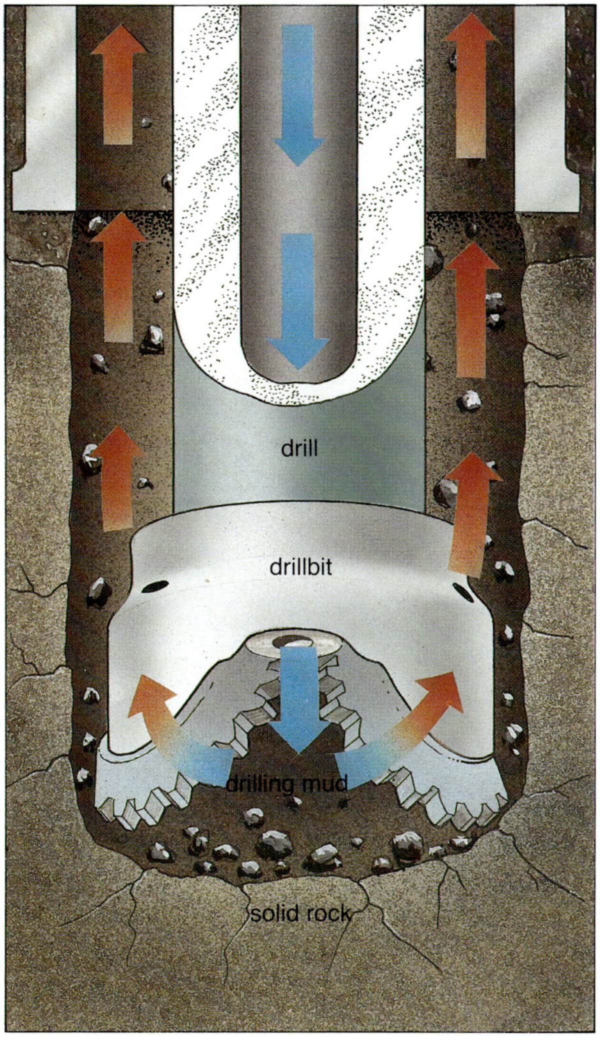

The line of drill pipes is called a **drill string**.
The part of the drill that digs into the ground is called the **drillbit**.
The workers pump **drilling mud** down the hollow drill pipes.
The drilling mud helps to keep the drillbit cool.
The drillbit cuts a deep hole in the solid rock.
The drilling mud rises up the hole, pushing up bits of rock to the surface.

Striking oil

When the oil underground is under great **pressure**, there is sometimes a **blowout**. The drillbit breaks through the rock. The pressure forces the oil and drilling mud up into the air.

The roughnecks work quickly to stop losing all the oil during a blowout. They fit a machine called a blowout preventer to the top of the drill pipe. The blowout preventer has a lot of **valves** which the roughnecks can open or shut to control the flow of liquid or gas in the drill pipe.

When the workers find oil, they take away the drill string and fit something called a 'Christmas tree' onto the well. The well is now ready to produce oil.

Our picture shows a 'Christmas tree' with a drilling rig in the background.

Natural gas

Natural gas is a mixture of gases which, like oil, are hydrocarbons.
Natural gas is often found in pockets above the oil in an oilfield.

a gas flare burning in North Africa

a temple to the fire god in Baku, in the USSR

this drilling rig burns the gas it does not need in a flare

Drilling rigs have a special pipe or **flare** for burning off the unwanted gas, but this is a waste of valuable energy. Scientists have now found ways to store the gas and send it by ship or pipeline to other countries.

Some countries have big gasfields. The largest gasfield in the world is in Siberia, in the USSR.

In some places gas leaks out from cracks in the Earth and catches fire. People thought the flames were a sign the gods were angry so they built temples to worship the god of fire.

Where oil and gas are found

Our map shows where the biggest fields of oil and natural gas are in the world.

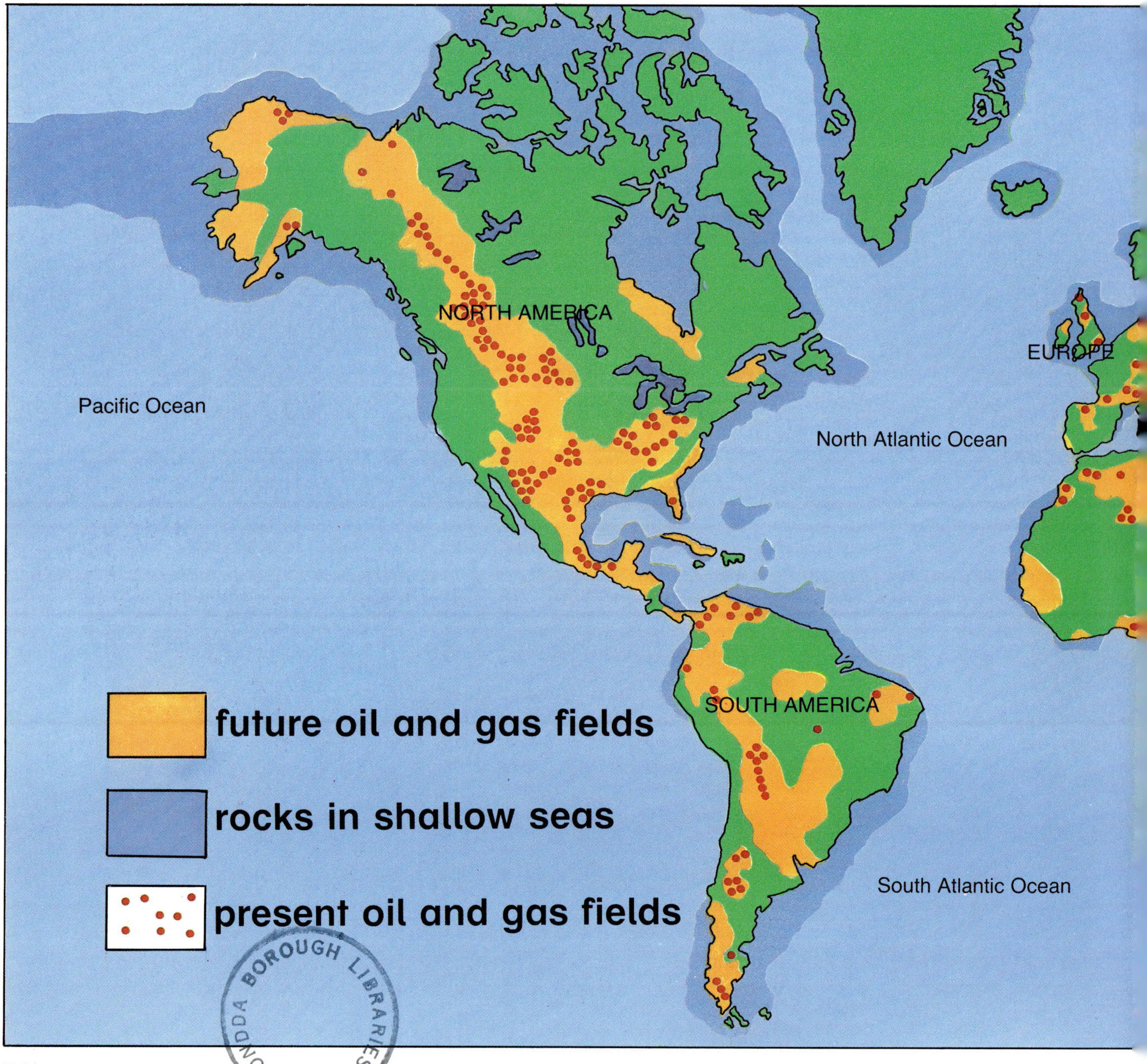

There are many more oil and natural gas fields than are shown by the red dots. Oil and gas are also found around the coasts in rocks under the shallow seas.

The world's biggest oil and gas fields are in places where few people live.

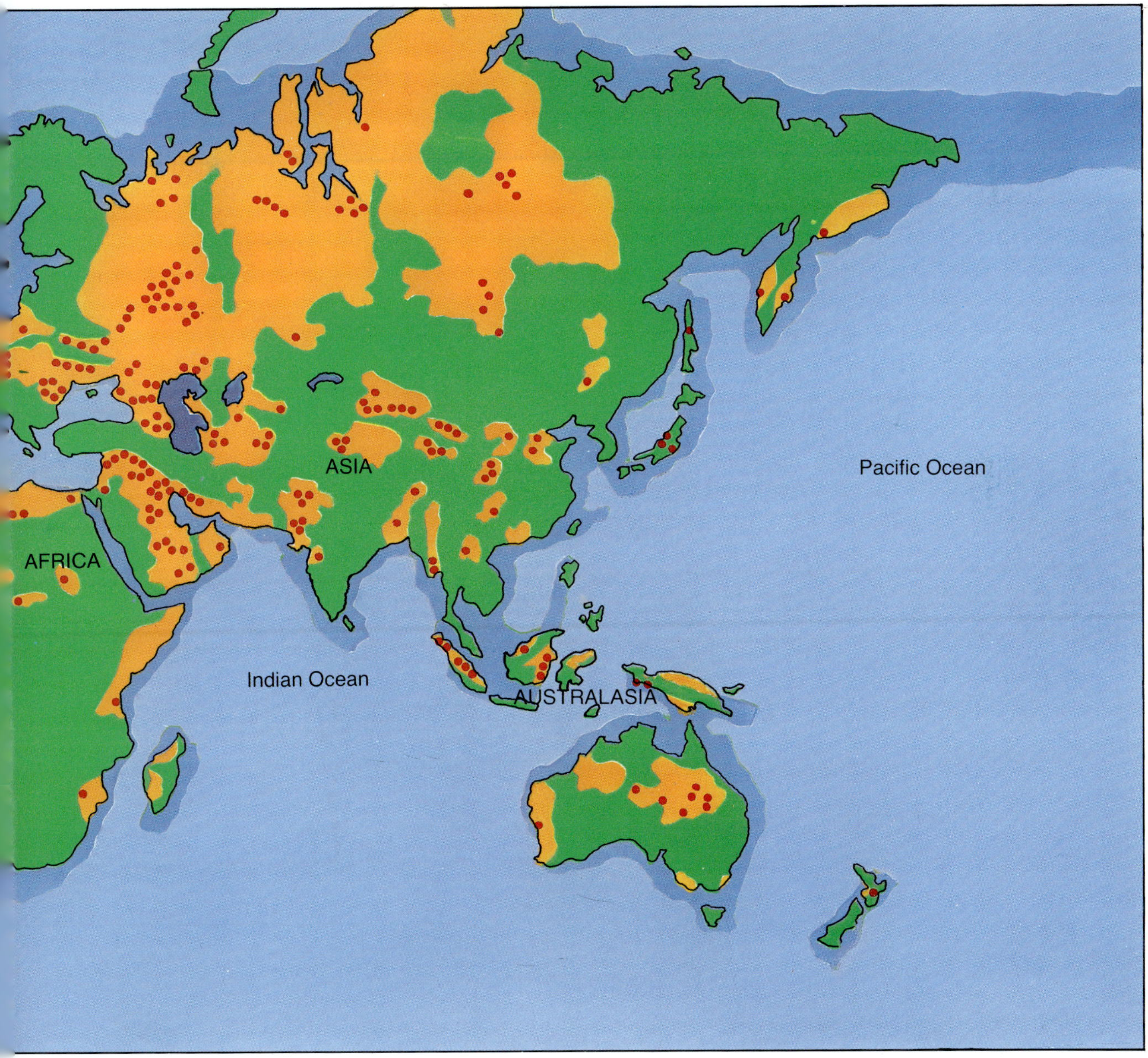

Oil and gas under the sea

When people began to want more oil for heating and **transport**, to power their factories and to make plastic goods, oil companies raised their prices. They also began to look for new oilfields in the sea.

Our picture shows an oil rig which drills for oil in the stormy North Sea between Britain and Norway.

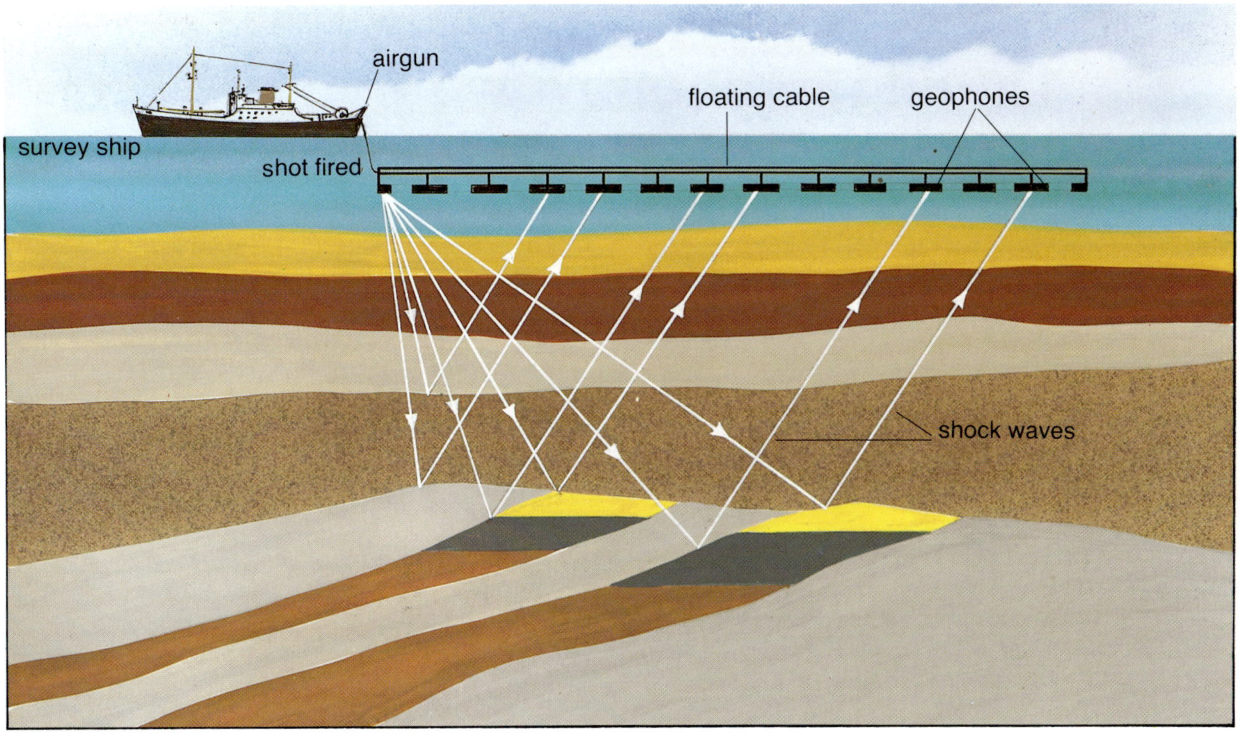

Scientists on survey ships can make seismic surveys of the ocean floor.
Airguns fixed to the back of the survey ship fire shots.
These send shock waves into rocks on the seabed.
The geophones which record the shock waves are tied to floating **cables** which are towed behind the ship.
The scientists on the ship measure the shock waves.

airguns and cables fixed to a survey ship

Drilling in shallow water

Some parts of the oceans are over 3000 metres deep.

The shallow seabed around the coast of every continent is called the **continental shelf**. This is usually only about 150 metres deep, so it is much easier to drill for oil on the continental shelf. The workers use **jack-up rigs** with long legs which can stand on the seabed.

The workers raise the legs when they tow the rig out to sea, and then lower them when they have reached the drilling site. When drilling is finished the workers raise the legs again and tow the rig to a new site.

Jack-up rigs can only be used in shallow water. Our diagram shows some other kinds of oil rigs. They are used to drill for oil under the sea in different depths of water.

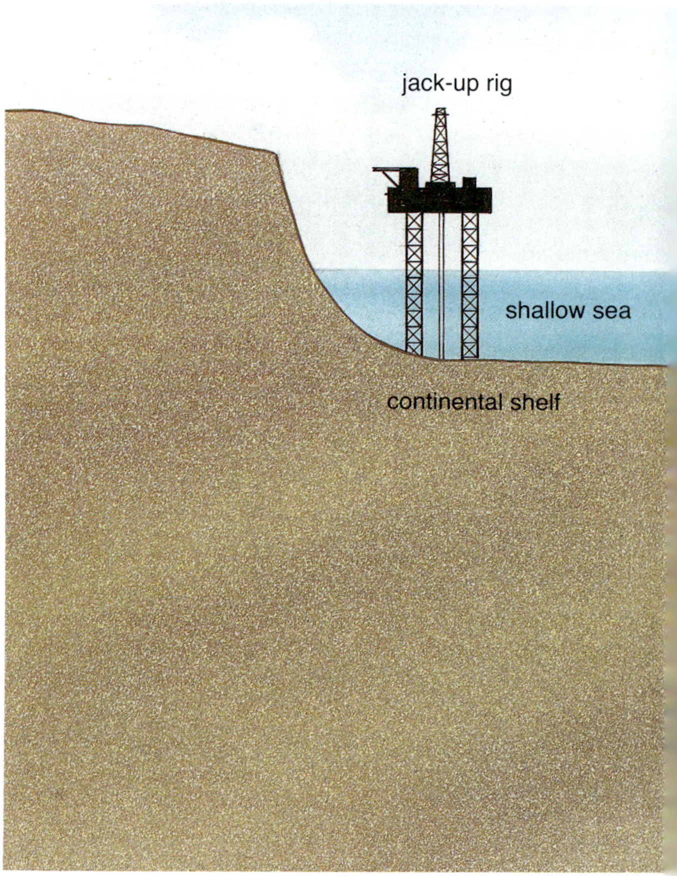

oil wells in Venezuela, 20 kilometres out to sea

Production platforms are made of steel or concrete. The legs of the platform are sunk into the seabed to make a strong fixed rig.

A **semi-submersible** rig is a large floating rig used in very deep water.

Drilling in deep water

Rigs in deep water have to be strong enough to stand up against high winds, tides and rough seas in bad weather.
Our picture shows a semi-submersible drilling rig.
Oil workers use this kind of rig to drill for oil in water which is between 50 and 500 metres deep.
The rig is towed to the drill site.

a semi-submersible rig

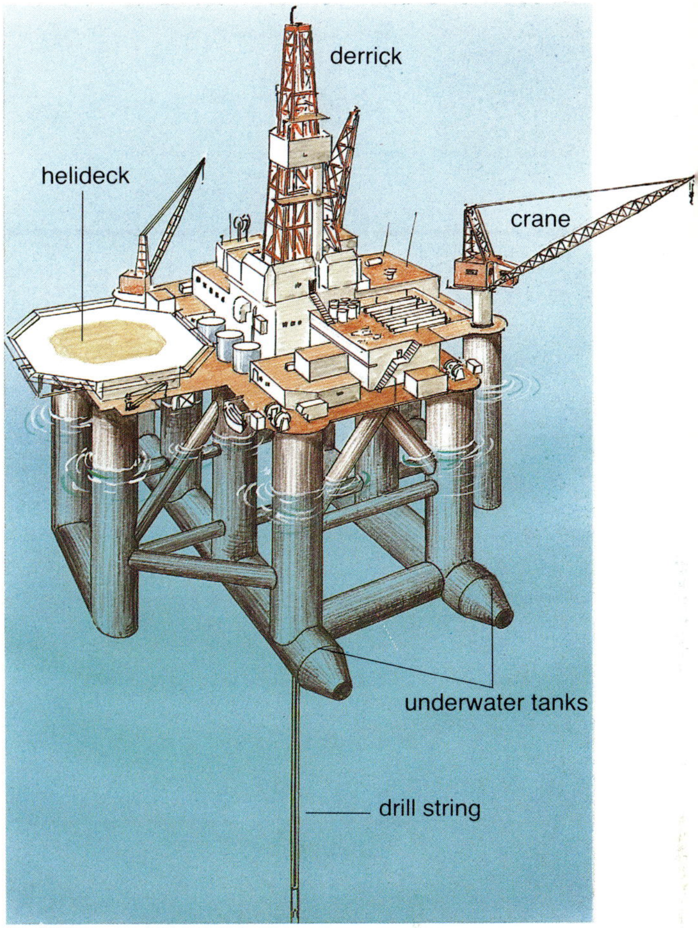

The rig has huge tanks which rest on the seabed in shallow water.
The weight of water in the tanks keeps the rig still.
In deeper water the rig floats like a ship.

Drill ships are used to drill in water up to one kilometre deep.
Computers on board keep the ship in position.

a drilling ship

A production platform

Our drawing shows an off-shore production platform.

1 The oil and gas flow up the pipes from the seabed.

2 The 'Christmas tree' controls the flow of oil.

3 Water and gas are taken out of the oil.

4 The oil is stored in tanks in the platform's legs.

5 Pumps send the gas along pipes to the shore.

6, 7, 8, & 9 The gas is treated and made safe to use.

10 Water pumps.

11 Gas and oil are used to make electricity.

12 Drilling rigs.

13 The flare tower burns off unwanted gas.

14 The landing deck for helicopters.

workers lay a pipeline in Texas in the United States

15 Lifeboat.

16 Bedrooms, dining rooms and a cinema for the workers.

17 The drilling deck has a special floor which allows the drilling rig to move.

The workers on the rig can take oil from a number of wells in the seabed. They drill as many as 20 or 30 wells from one platform. The workers drill straight down from the platform. They also drill at different **angles** away from the rig.

An offshore production platform

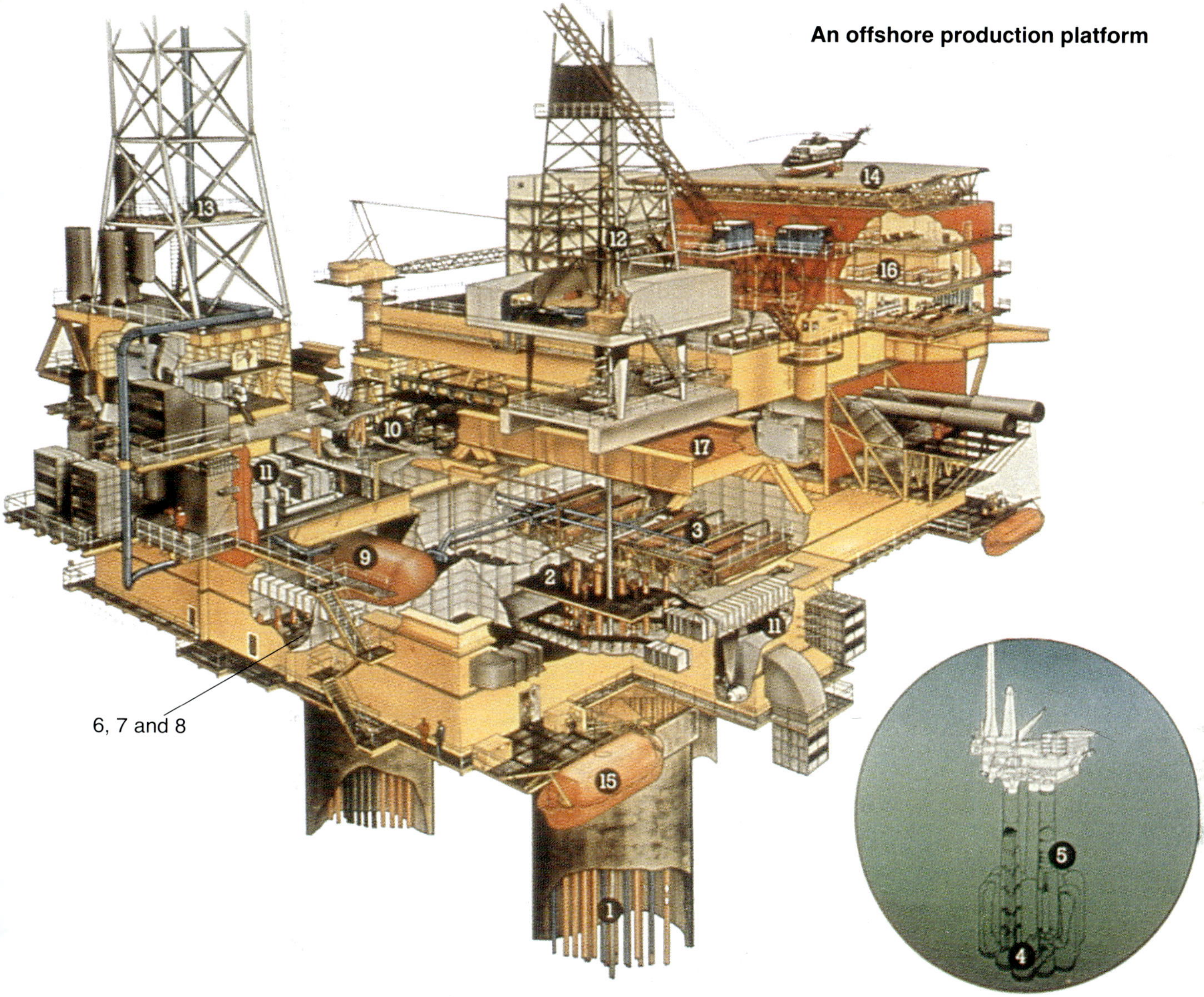

the huge *Brent B* production platform which was built in Norway and towed to an oilfield in the North Sea

Working at sea

Living on a production platform is like living in a small town in the middle of the sea.

There is not much space, so four workers have to share each bedroom.

It is also very noisy.

The drill rig clatters away all day and night.

Helicopters come and go, bringing in new staff and taking the workers back to the shore for their leave.

these men are working 20 metres above the sea

The men wear special overalls and hard hats for work out of doors.

helicopters bring fresh food and supplies

The workers stay on the rig for two to three weeks at a time.
They are well paid because the work is hard, boring and dangerous.

There are many different kinds of jobs on the rig.
Engineers check that the machinery is in good order.
Divers make sure that the parts of the platform under the sea are safe.
Radio operators keep in touch with the mainland.
Nurses and doctors take care of everyone's health.

The workers watch videos in their spare time.

divers working under the platform

Arctic oil

Oil workers in the Arctic have to drill through ice in the bitter cold. They have many problems because winter in the Arctic is long, cold and dark. When the temperature falls to $-60°$ C it is too cold for them to work and the machinery freezes up.

The Arctic Ocean is always frozen so ships cannot take the oil away.

this oil well on Spitsbergen is only 1000 kilometres from the North Pole

Workers built a pipeline from the north of Alaska to Valdez in the south where the ocean is not frozen. Now oil tankers can load up with oil all year round.

Drifting blocks of ice called **ice floes** can damage the Arctic oil rigs. Engineers from Japan and the United States designed an oil rig which can be used in the Arctic Ocean. It has a steel skirt which protects it from the ice.

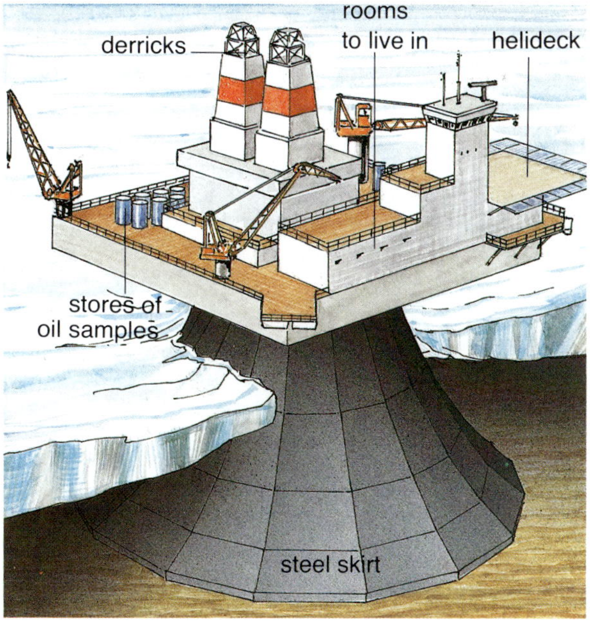

the new drilling rig

Submarines can take the oil away because they can move under the ice.

oil workers in Alaska must wear warm clothes against the bitter cold

Oil from sand and shale

Most of our oil comes from wells deep under the ground.
A lot of oil is also found in two kinds of rock just under the surface, called **oil sands** and **oil shale**.
Oil sands look like thick black gravel.
They are covered in a thick, sticky oil.
Our picture shows oil sands along the Orinoco River in South America.

Oil shale is found in the United States, the USSR, China and Scotland. Oil shale contains a hydrocarbon called **kerogen**. The oil shale is crushed and heated to 600°C. The kerogen in the shale turns into a gas which is cooled into a liquid oil. Oil from shale can be used in oil lamps.

In Trinidad, **pitch** lies on the surface of the ground. Our picture shows workers digging up solid pitch.

many years ago Scottish shale miners used pick axes to break up the rocks

Things we make from oil

Oil from an oil well must be treated in an **oil refinery** before it can be used.

The oil is heated to 350°C until it boils and gives off **vapour**.
The vapour is fed to a tall tower where it cools as it rises up the tower.
The hydrocarbons in the vapour turn to liquids at different temperatures.

Natural gas is treated before use, in gas plants like this one in our picture.

products from an oil refinery

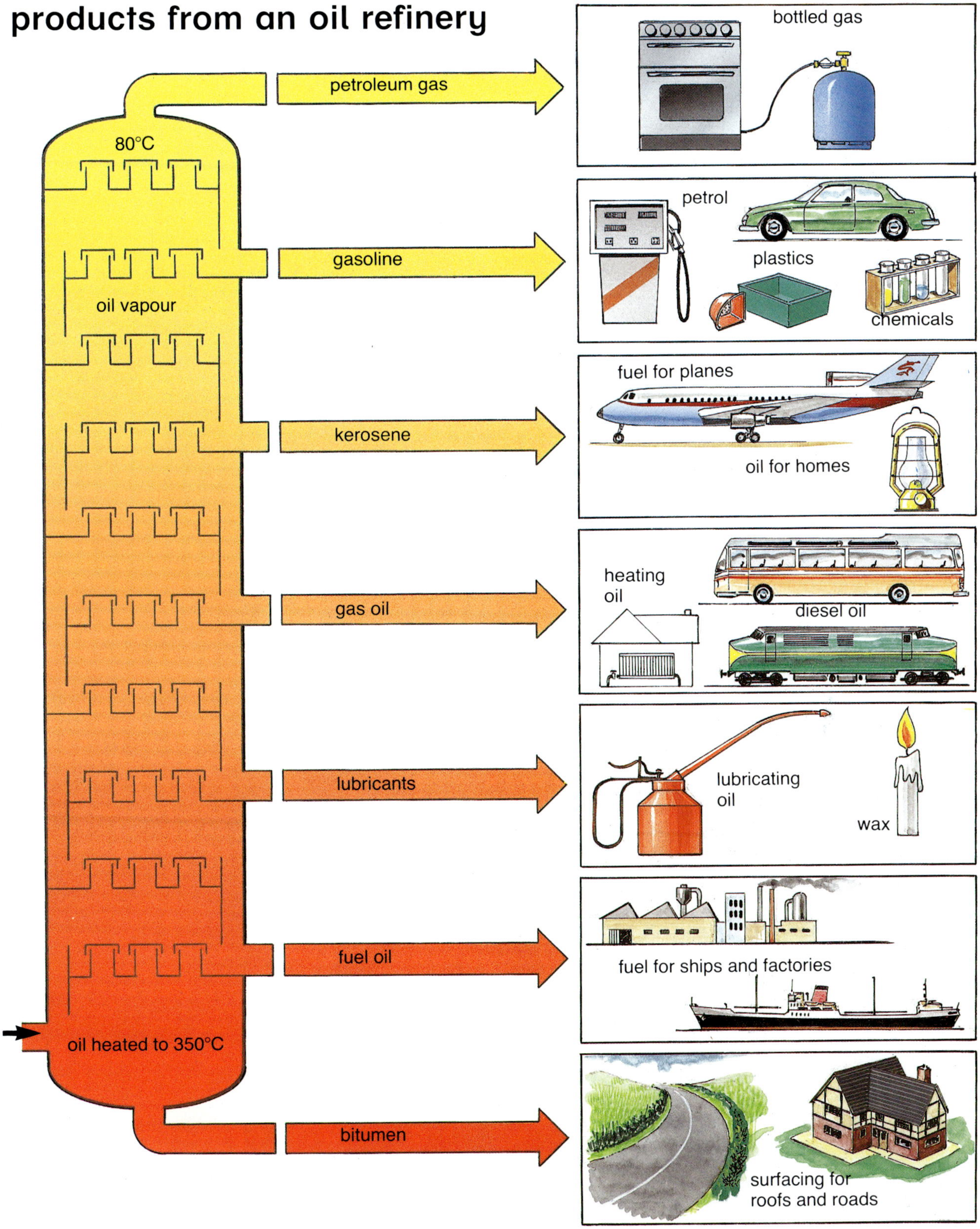

Using oil and gas

We use a lot of fossil fuels in our everyday lives.
We use gas for cooking and heating, petrol in our cars, **aviation** fuel in our planes, and diesel fuel in our trains and trucks.
All the machines in our homes, cars and factories need oil to make the parts move smoothly without **friction**.

all kinds of machines need oil

We use heating oil in our homes and offices and fuel oil in factories and ships. Chemicals and plastics are made from oil.
We use heavy black pitch and **bitumen** to cover the surface of our roads.

All fossil fuels took millions of years to make. In future we must try to **conserve** our stocks of fossil fuels.
Our diagram shows that unless we use less fossil fuels, we will run out of them very quickly.

a fuel pump in Brazil

Some countries like Brazil are already using alcohol in cars instead of petrol.

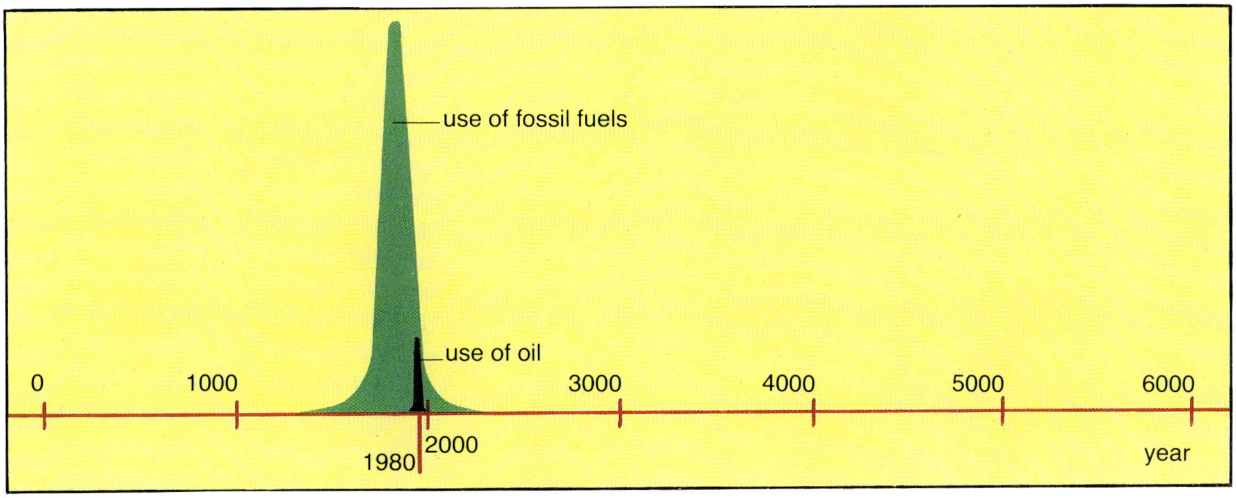

Oil and gas in the future

Our pictures show what our homes would look like without the plastics, floor and wall coverings, and other things which are made from oil.
Most of the world's oil is used in transport, to make cars and planes travel faster.

Scientists say that if we continue to use fossil fuels for energy there is only enough oil left for 35 years and enough gas for another 60 years.

Many people think we should use **renewable** energy such as wind and water power to make electricity instead of burning oil and gas as fuels.

scientists think we may be able to get more oil or gas from much deeper wells, or use the hot gases which come up from the very centre of the Earth

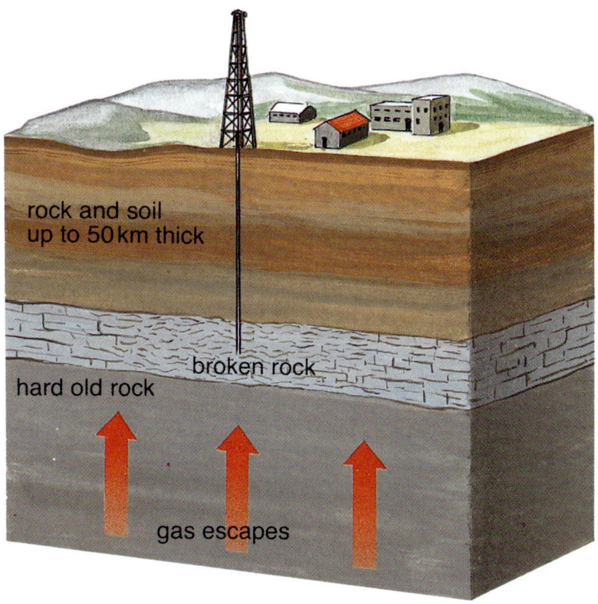

Glossary

angle not straight up and down, but slanting away from the rig

aviation to do with flying aircraft

bitumen a thick heavy oil used to make roofs and roads waterproof

blowout when oil gushes out from underground in an uncontrolled fountain

cables strong wires twisted together and used as ropes

carbon a chemical element found in fuels, foods and all living things

carbon dioxide a gas found in the air. Plants use carbon dioxide to make food

conserve to protect something and use it carefully

continental shelf a shallow seabed off the coast of a continent

derrick a tower made of steel which is built over an oil or gas well. Derricks are used to support the drilling equipment

drill a machine used to cut into rock

drill string a line of hollow pipes which surround the cutting part of the drill

drillbit the end of the drill which cuts through the rock

drilling mud a special chemical which is used to keep the drill cool and help it work well

drilling platform a large flat surface made of steel and concrete which supports the derrick

energy the power that makes things move and work

flare the flame that is made when the unwanted gas is burned off

fossil fuels materials that are made from the dead bodies of plankton. Fossil fuels like coal and oil are burned to produce energy

fossils the remains of an animal or plant, which are usually found in rocks

friction when two things rub together and wear each other away

geologists scientists who study rocks and the history of the Earth

geophones instruments which record the information about the shock waves in an underground test

hydrocarbons chemical compounds made up of hydrogen and carbon, which are found in coal, oil and natural gas

hydrogen a gas which is very light and burns easily

ice floes floating pieces of ice found in the Arctic and Antarctic Oceans

infra-red invisible rays which we feel as heat

jack-up rig a floating platform with legs which can be raised and lowered

kerogen the gas given off when oil shale is heated to 500°C

microwaves waves sent out by a machine which can pick out hydrocarbons in the air

oil refinery a factory which separates oil into a number of different fuels and chemicals

oil sands areas of gravel which hold large amounts of heavy oil

oil shale a hard rock containing oil

oxygen a gas found in air and water

pitch a thick solid oil found on the surface of the ground in some countries

pressure when something pushes hard down on something else

production platforms large platforms raised above sea level to hold an oil rig

renewable something that can be replaced or put back after being used

roughnecks skilled workers on an oil rig

satellite a small body in space that circles round a larger body or planet like Earth

seismic survey a way of finding out what kinds of rocks are under the surface by using a series of small explosions

semi-submersible a large floating oil rig which has tanks underneath it to keep it afloat

shock wave a wave made by an explosion or very fast movement

transport ways of getting from one place to another

valve a kind of tap which opens or closes to let water, fuel or gas pass in or out of a pipe

vapour tiny drops which form in the air when a liquid is heated

Index

Photographic credits
(t=top b=bottom l=left r=right)
cover: Science Photo Library/Richard Folwell; **title page:** Science Photo Library/David Parker
4 ZEFA; 6 Science Photo Library: 11, 12, 13 Shell UK; 15*b* Science Photo Library; 16, 17, 18 Shell Uk; 19 Hugh Jones/Seaphot; 20 Shell UK; 21, 22*t* ZEFA; 22*b* Novosti Press Agency; 23 ZEFA; 26, 27 Shell UK; 29 ZEFA; 30 Brian Coope/Seaphot; 31 British Petroleum; 32 ZEFA; 33 Shell UK; 34*t* John Lythgoe/Seaphot; 34*b* Chris Fairclough Picture Library; 35*t* Shell UK; 35*b* Jon Kenfield/Seaphot; 36 ZEFA; 37 British Petroleum; 38 Shell UK; 39*t* ZEFA; 39*b* British Petroleum; 40 Chris Fairclough Picture Library; 42 British Petroleum; 43 The Hutchinson Library